Democracy Made Safe

CW00551707

DEMOCRACY MADE SAFE

BY

PAUL HARRIS DRAKE

*" The old order changeth, yielding place to new; and God fulfills
Himself in many ways, lest one good custom should corrupt the world."*
TENNYSON

BOSTON
THE FOUR SEAS COMPANY
1920

Copyright, 1918, by

LeRoy Phillips

AUG 24 1933
HARVARD COLLEGE
LIBRARY

substituted for copy lost

The Four Seas Press
Boston, Mass., U. S. A.

TO
" MY CHILDREN'S CHILDREN "

" Ill fares the land, to hastening ills a prey,
  Where wealth accumulates and men decay."
                                    — *Goldsmith*.

FOREWORD

The desirability of reforming our social system so that "justice will flow down like water and righteousness like a mighty stream" is conceded by every right-thinking person today. In the minds of the vast majority of people our present method of doing business is far from satisfactory as a basis of human society. As a result, the world teems with every description of reform organization imaginable. The mere existence of such societies and bands of well-disposed persons is evidence of the fact that something is wrong.

How to go about the problem of readjusting society to conform with advanced ideals of humanity and social well-being is the thing which puzzles most people. "What shall we do to be saved?" is the well-nigh universal question. It is the purpose of the following pages to answer that question in a rational and humane spirit.

Much is heard in these days of "making the world safe for Democracy." To that end every right-thinking individual must consecrate himself wholeheartedly. But the war will be over one day, and, with the advent of a democratic peace will return the old problem of securing justice and right to the downtrodden of the earth. When Democracy in government is securely won the next great problem will be to make Democracy a living reality. The following pages are definitely concerned with the task of making Democracy safe for the world. If the winning of the world for Democracy is to be permanent it can never rest on the old foundations of competitive capitalism. Only by boldly taking the step outlined herein will Democracy be made safe in the opinion of the writer.

No one needs to be told of the vast changes which have been sweeping over the industrial life of the world since the discovery of electricity and steam as motive forces. It is sufficient to say that the entire agricultural and industrial basis of human society has been transformed during the past one hundred years. And history tells us in unmistakable terms that industrial revolution is inevitably followed by corresponding changes in the thought and habits of those who happen to be affected thereby. Therefore, because of the tremendous industrial revolution which we have been undergoing since the year 1800, we ought logically to expect a political and social revolution of corresponding moment. Nothing else is to be expected. How to meet it and subdue it to our requirements as a social whole is the pressing problem.

Many, if not all, of our social ills and evils are due to the failure of our social and political thinking to keep pace with, or abreast of, our industrial, commercial and financial thinking. If we are logical and read history with insight we ought to expect ideas in the realm of political and social progress to be fully as revolutionary as in the field of industrial, commercial and financial improvement.

Most people are prone to believe that social relations and customs are fixed for all time, and that industrial and commercial methods are alone susceptible to improvement. Nothing could be farther from the truth. Change and flux are quite as much the rule of social and political relations as of industrial and commercial progress. And while such progress is never of uniform or even growth in the material fields of endeavor, the same is true also of progress in the social and political realms.

In nature long periods of incubation are followed by the often catastrophic and revolutionary phenomena of birth. Yet in such cases the sudden appearance of new forms of life springing from the vitality and nurture of the parent stock are but normal processes of evolution advanced by apparent revolution. The same thing is true of many mechanical inventions which embody many a well-known principle, yet which, nevertheless, are strikingly new. Might it not be that social growth follows the same laws as biological and mechanical growth?

The reader should bear constantly in mind that it is not revolution which is harmful to society, but the thwarting of it that works dire results. Some things are bound to take place in the ordinary course of events. When any blind obstructionist gets in the way of the normal fulfilment of certain clearly defined social movements, something is likely to happen. One of two things must happen: either the obstruction is pushed ruthlessly aside or trampled upon, or, the on-rushing stream of human tendency is pushed from its normal course to crop out in other directions.

The world on which we live, scientists tell us, is constantly revolving. The earth must, because of its nature, rotate upon itself and at the same time revolve about the sun. Revolution, in other words, is the first principle of permanent stability. We are safe so long as revolution occurs in an orderly and systematic fashion. But let anything interfere with the ordained revolution of the earth and unimaginable catastrophe would result. We ought not to be afraid of revolution in human affairs. Rather should we concern ourselves as to the failure of revolution to take place as scheduled, and remove the causes which impede the orderly operation of social changes.

The discovery of steam and electricity both occasioned a revolution in industry. The invention of many well-known labor-saving devices likewise caused an equal number of industrial revolutions. The utilization of certain improved mechanical devices causes corresponding industrial revolutions today. Why, then, should we in our thinking set our minds against social and political revolutions, which are as much ordained by the powers that be as are the orbits of the stars? Our unwillingness or inability to adjust ourselves to the changes which have been, and are, taking place is the cause of most of our trouble and confusion.

It is just as unprogressive to have eighteenth-century ideas in your head as it is to have eighteenth-century equipment on your farm or in your business. Most people will purchase the latest improved implement or device for use in their business, but are perfectly content to worry along as best they may with obsolete and unworkable social and political conceptions of humanity. The inconsistency of such established procedure is too well known to require elucidation.

Many a business man whose social conceptions are as hoary as Methuselah immediately goes to great expense whenever a labor-saving invention is placed upon the market in order to be "up to date" and "efficient" in his business. Yet the same business man will not spend two cents — or a few hours' time (which is more important) — to inform himself regarding the changes which have taken place in philosophy and thought during the past decade even. "Millions for equipment, but not one cent for thought" appears to be the slogan of the successful men of affairs everywhere.

With a view to stimulating thought toward a definite end this book is written. That end appears to the writer to be the next and greatest step forward which humanity has yet taken in its upward climb. Nothing less than the total abolition of all forms of money and capitalistic enterprise is demanded. The reason for this demand, and the wisdom of it, is to be found in the following pages. The perusal of these pages is especially commended to those whose ready answer to such a sweeping proposal is, "It can't be done."

CONTENTS

" New times demand new measures and new men;
The world advances, and in time outgrows
The laws that in our fathers' day were best;
And, doubtless, after us, some purer scheme
Will be shaped out by wiser men than we,
Made wiser by the steady growth of truth."

— *James Russell Lowell.*

CHAPTER I

THE PROPOSITION

The business of the world will one day be run without the medium of money. The time will come when all of the present indispensable mediums of exchange will not exist. Not until that time comes will Democracy be assured.

Have you never marvelled at the dexterity of the quick and accurate cashier and thought, "What a waste of energy! How much better off the world would be if such cleverness could be utilized in some creative effort!"

Did you ever stand in awe before the working of a highly trained and specialized office force and say to yourself, "What a pity that so many good men and women should work to no purpose! What a volume of useful and necessary commodities these people could be producing if their pains and energy were directed to some worthier end!"

Waste. When you stand in line before a store counter and wait impatiently for the tired clerk to carefully weigh out your purchases and jot each item down on a slip of paper, have you never thought "How puerile — how simply childish that I should be compelled to suffer all this rigmarole in order to secure a few varieties of necessary food!" Did it ever occur to you that all clerks, bookkeepers, accountants, cashiers and bankers engaged in the handling and care of money were a useless drag on the productivity of society and ought to be engaged in better business?

Consider for a moment the army of anemic indoor workers in white collars and cuffs — women as well as men — who ought to be out of doors in the bright sunshine engaged in wholesome creation and recreation. Wouldn't it be a blessing for them, if, instead of wasting their lives in assisting others to amass a fortune, they could partake of some of the joys and privileges of living now enjoyed only by the wealthy and leisure classes?

The End of Labor. The same consideration applies to all other classes of our working population. The end of labor is what labor begets — play, leisure, joy, possession. Simply to work for the sake of working, while it might conceivably keep one out of mischief, is not the end of human existence.

How can society secure for all humanity fit to be at large a greater measure of the joys and happinesses of life? This question ought to be the all-absorbing topic of discussion everywhere and at all seasons.

THE TRAGEDY OF LIVING

The end of human existence is LIFE — always and forever more life. In a world of wonders most people are born, live and die within a few miles of their little corner of the earth, "unwept, unhonored and unsung." Few indeed ever live to know from observation anything worth knowing about all the natural and created beauties of the world into which they are born.

This is a fearful thing. It is little short of hideous to think of the possibilities of life and then to consider how few are permitted to develop or to enjoy one-half of the possibilities which life affords.

With a little careful thinking it becomes increasingly plain that the chief obstacle to a richer, more abundant life for all human beings is our woeful lack of co-ordination and co-operation. On every hand we have abundant evidence of man's creative genius. There is no lack of witnesses to the potential power of man to rise above his natural environment.

The Need. The thing which alone is lacking

is a comprehensive, common-sense view of human society as a whole. Once men arrive at a truly social view of life, the glaring anomalies of our present social system appear foolish and intolerable.

So long as we permit mere avarice and covetousness to run riot in society, just so long will we be compelled to tolerate the injustices and inequalities which now corrode and disintegrate.

Many people, shorn of all illusions by their experience of life, soberly question the worth of living in a condition where deception and insincerity are the common routine of existence. What value is there in living where people, even if of the so-called successful classes, must endure the sight and sound of their brothers in bondage? It were hell and little else to be harnessed forever to grossness and bestiality in a world like ours so full of possibility and promise.

Who Will Solve It?

Well may the one to whom has come a sense of the enormity of such conditions exclaim with Paul of Tarsus, "Who shall separate me from this body of death?" Of course, the answer to this heart-rending plea is very simple. "No one but ourselves." Only the collective common sense of men and women is able to save society from its downward tendencies. Nothing else availeth anything.

The one thing perhaps above any other which has thus far held the world in bondage is the lack of vision of its alleged great men. Either that, or there has never been a sufficient number of far-sighted men to persuade the world of the reasonableness of their point of view.

The Promise. At all events the world is moving rapidly these days and men are beginning to realize that nothing of which the human mind can conceive is finally impossible. The Deity does not give men conceptions of things without the possibility of their eventual fulfilment. This does not mean that every harebrained scheme which enters the heads of people is necessarily a panacea for all the ills to which flesh is heir. Far from it.

What it does mean is that every well-considered, soberly conceived, and rational plan of human improvement is bound to be fulfilled provided people will see the way clear and work to that end.

Hitherto men on this planet have been largely blind pawns moved about by the inscrutable hand of fate. Men have not understood "the manner of spirit they were of." Confusion and blindness have resulted.

A New View. Today, for the first time in the history of the world, men are beginning to see and understand the forces by which human destiny is shaped, and to struggle to take the trowel in their own hands. Instead of being driven by blind forces, mankind is struggling to gain possession of the reins wherewith to direct human progress and attainment.

The entire point of view of thoughtful men has changed from theocentric to homocentric. Henceforth men are to be the arbiters of their own destinies. And there is no question but what the deliberate decisions of humanity as a whole will be realized.

How men will act on broad general plans for their own emancipation and advantage, once clearly understood, history records. When men once become imbued with the justice and desirability of an idea they will move heaven and earth in its accomplishment. Life on this planet would be a sorry and complete failure if this were not so.

Its Simplicity. The more simple a thing, the easier it is grasped by any large number of people. To be successful, a plan for social regeneration must carry with it the assurance that it will do the things which are claimed for it. When such a plan is sufficiently simple to be immediately understood by any and all to whom it is broached, and when such a plan appeals to the good sense of mankind as presenting a flawless and desirable *modus operandi* for the securing of all the essentials and many of the luxuries of life — when it fulfils these two conditions there is every reason to hope for its adoption.

PRESENT CONDITIONS

Such a programme and such a *modus operandi* are herewith indicated.

So long as mutual confidence prevails it is a matter of common experience that an individual or a corporation can continue to do business long after the interchange of money has ceased. Credit of thirty, sixty, ninety or more days is a common thing in the world of modern business.

Just so long as a person or a firm is believed to be solvent they can secure credit in a reasonable amount. It doesn't matter if the bills remain unpaid for months even at a time in some instances. If the creditor knows the debtor is good for the amount of his bill he will continue to extend his credit up to an often extraordinary figure. The creditor, in turn, as it often happens, goes in debt for commodities to sell to the debtor in the belief that he will sooner or later get his investment back at a profit.

Confidence. So long as the creditor's confidence is not misplaced, all goes well. Both debtor and creditor in turn continue to live with their accustomed expenditure, and, so long as the bills are met and the notes paid on the stipulated days of reckoning, things go along without a hitch.

What good reason is there to suppose that if no one ever paid his bills, and everybody continued to do his work as usual, such credit could not be extended indefinitely? And everybody be as serenely happy as if the actual money represented had been paid? Here is the germ thought upon which depends the future economic status of human society. How soon will men develop the requisite faith to enter upon such a condition? That is an altogether different question.

When Will Money End?

But the time is surely coming when nothing in the form of money or any medium of exchange will be necessary in the transaction of the world's business. Sufficient and to spare will one day be produced for all mankind. Many are not so sure but that day has not already arrived. When abundance for every human need is possible for all, then will the interchange of money of every sort come to an end.

Men can do much to hasten that day, although such a day will come at length whether men do anything consciously to hasten the day or not.

What lies within the province of human endeavor to make for the speedy consummation of this prophecy? This is the immediate question.

Consider for a moment the millions of people engaged in occupations which are conditioned upon, and minister only to, the accumulation of private fortunes. Reflect on the myriads of bookkeepers, cashiers, accountants, clerks, stenographers, agents, traveling salesmen, bankers and brokers!

An Abundance of Labor. Suppose that these quick-witted, intelligent people who are numbered by the million, and who comprise probably a tenth of the people who earn their living, were set free from such occupation and added to the producers of the world! Suppose, with the abolition of rents, dividends and interest, a few million more people, who now do nothing whatever for the common weal, would be forced to join the ranks of the industrial armies of the world! Suppose several million lawyers, preachers, butlers, flunkies and others engaged in personal service were to hear the call of Democracy to the extent of doing something creative for a living — what a wealth of labor would be freed for constructive, useful employment!

Abundant Product. Then let the superior wisdom of great captains of industry put these able-bodied people to work creating economic wealth in abundance. Who is there so stupid as to doubt that our present industrial army, reinforced by such a brigade — augmented by the return of 40,000,000 soldiers to the pursuits of peace — would be shortly able to produce such a wealth of commodities of every variety that every last man, woman and child on the face of the earth could partake freely — without money and without price — and there would still remain vast stores of unused food, clothing and building materials?

Objections

Objections to such a radical procedure? There aren't any of any consequence. If one man is enabled to have all he wants — all he can use — (as there will then be no market in which to sell anything) what cares he if his neighbor has enough and to spare? It makes no difference to me what my brother has so long as I have everything I desire. Simple enough, isn't it?

It may be that you are still in doubt. "How do you know that such a volume of goods of every kind and description would result? Where's your proof?" you ask!

CHAPTER II

THE PROOF

The proof is in the fact that already, were it not for the purely artificial stimulus occasioned by the war, business stagnation would be a continuous condition.

With scientific methods, coupled with the vastly increased productivity of modern industrial processes, economic goods are produced much faster than they can be consumed in times of peace. Chronic underconsumption — miscalled "overproduction" — has been with us, lo, these many years.

Financial Panics. The frequently recurring periods of industrial depression — the so-called business panics of recent years — are living witnesses to the truth of this contention. Have we forgotten the memorable winter of early 1915 when 5,000,000 industrial workers were on the streets clamoring for bread? Soup kitchens, bread lines and Hotel de Ginks are a recent memory in our industrial civilization.

So long as wages in the aggregate continue to fall short of the total value of all commodities produced, chronc underconsumption is bound to result. So long as the combined purchasing power of all classes of society never equals the retail prices asked for the entire product of industry there must remain an unconsumed margin of goods. As nearly 80 per cent of the buying power of society is represented by the overwhelming number of middle and lower-class individuals in the world, it is plain that these are the people to whom capital looks for a market for the bulk of its products.

Underconsumption. But, owing to the low average wage — which means a low average consumption — these people are permitted to consume but a fraction of that which their labor produces. As a result, surplus economic wealth in the shape of accumulated food stuffs, clothing, shoes and luxuries is left high and dry without a purchaser. For the remaining 20 per cent of the population — in spite of their great wealth and luxurious living, in spite of their love of extravagance and display — are quite unable to consume the great volume of unsold commodities. A struggle for foreign markets in which to sell the unconsumed surplus is the logical result.

"Made in Germany." When the foreign markets have absorbed all their limited wealth can

pay for, business ceases — hoist by its own
petard. So Germany — perhaps the most glaring example of over-ripe capitalism — desiring
a larger foreign market for her surplus wealth,
deliberately began a world-war.

Under our antiquated form of doing business,
all enterprise ceases when there is no market.
It matters not whether people are hungry and
without sufficient clothing to keep warm. They
must starve and freeze until capital can see a
profit in employing them again. Of all the
paradoxes of capitalism this condition is the
most stupid and inane.

Curtailing Production

Merchants even seek to withhold products
from the consumer in order to create an artificial scarcity so that prices will advance. Re-
stricted output is often resorted to for the
purpose of keeping up prices. Occasionally
great quantities of food stuffs are deliberately
dumped and left to rot because the market does
not happen to be "right" for the owner of such
foods to sell at a sufficient profit.

Each autumn when people in the cities are
dying for lack of the acid fruits so necessary to
complete nutrition, whole orchards are left un-
picked of their fruit because there isn't sufficient
profit incentive to make it worth while to
harvest such crops. Where can the brains of a

civilization be which will complacently countenance such conditions?

Must shoe-workers go barefoot because they have produced too many shoes? Must bakers go hungry because they have baked too much bread? Shall carpenters be compelled to go without a roof because they have built too many houses? The absurdity of our present method of doing business is an endless indictment of the wisdom and humanity of our alleged civilization.

Is further proof necessary to establish the validity of the assertion that modern industrial methods, if allowed unrestricted scope, are capable of producing food, clothing and shelter in abundance for everyone? As it is — with all of the anomalies of the present planless and chaotic system — everybody is provided for after a fashion. And, in peace times, an unconsumed balance of economic goods periodically results.

Feasibility of the New

Imagine what an increase in both the volume and quality of production would result if two-thirds again as many workers as are now actual producers were released from non-productive and useless occupations and put to work doing something really constructive! Does any one doubt that present-day society is capable of producing sufficient economic wealth so that every member of society could have everything necessary to live this life to its fullest and no one be compelled to go without anything necessary to subserve his highest welfare?

If any one is still skeptical as to the potential power of society to produce an abundance of everything (possessed as society is of such wonderful machinery), a few facts taken from the 1910 Census will not be amiss.

WHAT THE LAST CENSUS SHOWED

In 1916, out of a population of approximately 92,000,000 souls, we had 38,167,336 persons over ten years of age engaged in gainful occupations. The gainful workers of all kinds formed 41.5 per cent of the total population.

Of the total population, 29,000,000 were under 15 years of age, and 6,000,000 of the population were over 60 years old. Leaving out of account for practical purposes the 35,-000,000 children and aged persons included in the above, we have left a population of 57,-000,000 souls from whom are drawn the 38,000,000 or so of workers mentioned above.

Of course, a limited number of children between ten and fifteen years of age are included in the total number of workers given, Hence the figures cited for the number of children under fifteen include 1,990,225 child workers.

And the 6,000,000 aged persons (over 60) also include some workers. It would seem to be a fair guess that the number of child-workers under 15 and the number of adult workers over 60 years of age might total about 2,000,000. This 2,000,000 workers under 15 and over 60 are more than offset, for purposes of comparison, by the number of students between those ages in school and college.

Now to analyze our 57,000,000 or so of adults between the ages of 15 and 60:

Numbers in Certain Occupations

Of that number, 12,600,000 were engaged in Husbandry and Forestry; 1,000,000 in mining, 10,600,000 in all forms of manufacturing, 2,600,000 in transportation, 2,000,000 in professional and public service, making in all 28,800,000 persons more or less directly employed in necessary public service through production, distribution, and useful occupation.

In addition there were 3,600,000 people in "trade," 3,800,000 in "personal and domestic service," and 1,700,000 in "clerical" occupations. Of the 38,000,000 people employed in gainful occupations we see that approximately 29,000,000 of the population were engaged in actually essential pursuits and about 9,000,000 in more or less mere money-making occupations.

The "Necessary" Workers. So we have less

than 30,000,000 actually necessary workers in the United States to feed, clothe and shelter a population of 92,000,000 people!

We must not lose sight of the fact that this 29,000,000 of more or less necessary workers are in idleness about 20 per cent of the time in so-called "normal" years, and further, that of this 29,000,000 workers a substantial percentage are engaged in the manufacture and transportation of absolutely unnecessary and superfluous commodities. All such considerations enter into the final decision as to whether present-day society is potentially able to produce enough and to spare of every necessary commodity for every one.

SMALL PERCENTAGE OF ACTUAL PRODUCERS

With less than one-third of the population at work in useful pursuits in normal times, this one-third produced "enough to go round" for the other 29,000,000 adults of working age and for 35,000,000 children and aged persons as well!

And of the 29,000,000 actually employed in 1910 in creating and handling the things demanded by a wasteful, unscientific and vainglorious capitalism, it is well within the bounds of moderation to say that at least another 9,000,000 were employed in the production and distribution of things which are of use only

under a capitalistic competitive system — and
which would have absolutely no place in a well-
regulated system of co-operative endeavor! It
requires far less workers to produce what
people actually need, than the vast number who
are at present employed in producing commodities simply for profit.

The Net Result. After eliminating that part
of the population engaged in trivial and useless
production which is demanded only by capitalism, and after allowing for the percentage of
forced unemployment which is an intrinsic
concomitant of the existing order, is it not true
that only about 15,000,000 people would be
required at steady labor from day to day,
working eight hours a day, to produce and
distribute all of the commodities necessary for
the comfort, health and happiness of everybody
in the United States?

THE CONCLUSION

If this is so (and the author believes it to be
the fact), does any one seriously doubt the
ability of the whole population, of today not
less than 105,000,000, to produce such an
abundance of every conceivable commodity
that enough and to spare for every single
individual could be had from the joint product
of society, scientifically managed, resulting
from a five-hour workday?

A Five-Hour Day. As long ago as 1910, Mr. Carroll D. Wright, secretary of the United States Department of Labor, declared that if every adult male in this country actually worked at useful employment five hours a day five days in the week, the world's work — at least that portion of it which falls to the United States — would be done and done successfully. Is there a soul with brains so dead as to seriously question the validity of this assertion?

SUPERFLUOUS COMMODITIES

An enormous share of our modern effort centers around the necessity providing the accessories with which present business is transacted. A great amount of labor and thought is spent in producing many things which would be required but little or not at all under the régime which is ahead.

Consider what an infinite amount of energy and effort is required to produce simply the things which expedite the handling of commodities and the accompanying accounts occasioned by modern enterprise. What an army of well-trained and efficient producers would be liberated for the production of actual necessities under the plan advocated.

Today millions of people are engaged in the manufacture of scales, weighing apparatus, typewriters, adding machines, calculating devices, addressographs, mimeographs, stenotypes, cash registers, cost systems, accounting and filing systems, bookkeeping machines, blank books, safes, office appliances and furnishings which, while indispensable to the transaction of present-day business by private individuals, would be used in part or not at all under the system of unstinted production and joint proprietorship which is bound to come.

WHAT COULD BE ELIMINATED

Cash registers, counter scales, office safes, and all complicated machinery having to do with the recording of sales and the handling of money could be immediately abolished under the form of enterprise here outlined.

Typewriters for purely private business purposes, bookkeeping machines, ledgers, filing systems and many other office appliances and business accessories so common under privately owned, money-making business enterprises, would be reduced to a minimum under a system which did away with the present childish and stupid duplication of effort and competitive insanity.

One is staggered by the thought that the millions engaged in simply providing the machinery by which present-day "business" functions, would all find better and more useful employment under the new order of society. But this is exactly what is going to happen as soon as men become aware of the awful waste and inefficiency of present business methods. By getting rid of money and every incentive to accumulate money, the race will gain immeasurably.

What a wealth of taste and energy now used to no good purpose would be liberated for fine endeavor with the abolition of window trimming, showy display of saleable goods, advertising, unsightly car signs, billboards, fancy boxes, expensive wrappings, tinsel, tissue-paper and twine!

The almost bewildering diversity of schemes to catch the eye and the money of gullible purchasers would be eliminated forever. Millions of now employed but unserviceable people would be freed for useful, constructive and beneficent labor under the programme of a society which produced for use and not for profit.

A SPIRITUAL CONSIDERATION

Could anything be more spiritually belittling and mentally dwarfing than the thoughts now prevailing in millions of minds: "The work I do is of no real account in the world. The thing I am hired to do does nobody any good. I am not a producer of anything worth while. If I

should die my life has been spent almost for
nothing. I have added nothing to the sum-
total of the world's progress or efficiency. I
have not helped to liberate men from their
bondage to mere things. I have been merely a
cog in a machine to grind out profit for my
employer whose business is to traffic in the
pride, vanity and unworthy attributes of men
and women. I have lived to no purpose. My
life's work is of such a nature that it has no
permanent value to anybody. I am just a good-
for-nothing slave to my employer's interest
which, in turn, is a form of bondage to the
parasitical classes of society."

A Sad Admission. I repeat: with thoughts
like these, or the truths which spring from
them at any rate — what has life to offer to the
inarticulate millions engaged in trivial, incon-
sequential and unproductive forms of labor?
It were a thousand times better never to have
been born than to be born to a realization that
your work — the most important part of your
existence — plays no useful part in the economy
of the world.

THE LIFE WORTH WHILE

Nothing makes life more worth living than
to feel that what you are doing is important
to the world of which you are a part. Rob
endeavor of the conviction that it is insepa-

rably associated with great principles, great necessities, great ambitions, great yearnings or great anticipations and you make of work an empty husk — a hollow mockery. Yet how few today can say in the depths of their hearts: "The labor by which I earn my daily bread is of vital importance to the happiness and well-being of men." The inability of every last worker in the world to say the above sincerely and devoutly is in itself sufficient to indict our present society as cruel, soul-destroying and brutalizing in the extreme. Our social system will never be wholesome until every worker is able to say with sincerity: "The work I do is, above everything else, necessary to the world's highest good."

A Glaring Example. One of the most striking examples of the inability of private business enterprise to fulfil the demands of either capital or labor is the street-railway system of a certain eastern city.

Here is a great transportation system which already finds itself unable to give good service, pay its employees a living wage, or pay the customary dividends to its stockholders. The public which depends upon the railway system is neither able nor willing to pay an increase of fares for the inferior service which it receives.

The public is always willing to pay well for excellent service. That is another trait of human nature. It knows when it is well treated. But the public is not willing to stand for a raise of fares under present conditions of service rendered.

Service Only. So long as the present anomalous capitalistic system remains the public can and will afford to pay for actual service from the transportation companies. But the public cannot afford to pay for anything but transportation. The cost of "doing business" (aside from the cost of transportation) is the thing which has put the street-railway business of the country where it is today. The public served by the great transportation companies cannot and will not pay for an incubus of business pride, financial crookedness, legislative corruption and mismanagement. While the public stands ready to pay for the legitimate cost of actual transportation it has neither the money nor the patience to be taxed for the additional cost of that useless "impedimenta" demanded by present-day financial undertakings.

"Impedimenta"

In other words, the public cannot afford to pay the salaries of that great body of officials and employees engaged not in carrying passengers, but in making the railroads "pay."

Ticket sellers, ticket takers, auditors, lawyers, watchmen, policemen, gate-tenders, conductors, and their like in no way add to a street railway's efficiency, while they all serve to increase the "operating costs" tremendously. These people are not engaged in serving the public. They are employed to serve the company's directors in making money for the stockholders. That is all they are paid for, and that is their sole function. There is no good reason why the burden of this additional group of money jugglers and profit takers should be paid for out of the public's purse.

Even under the present system it would be the part of wisdom to send all of these employees not actually engaged in transportation, packing, and, allowing the public the free use of the entire street railway system with no more restrictions than are imposed upon users of the public highways, meet the bill for actual service rendered out of the public funds raised by taxation. Such a solution — even under the institution of private capitalism — would give the public better service for less money.

Does any one think for a moment that such a solution would not be feasible? At all events, the existing system of using a public-service franchise to make money for a small group of stockholders has been proven distinctly unworkable. Anything is preferable to the present intolerable conditions.

With the cutting out of all the complicated

and intricate machinery demanded by the necessity of "doing business," the cost of operating the average transportation system could be nearly cut in halves at one stroke. It would be a deal less expensive to the public to be taxed a little additional for the privilege of free and unrestricted transportation, than to be obliged to pay the present — or an increased — rate for very inferior accommodations. Who would not prefer to suffer an increase in the tax rate of, say, a dollar a thousand, than be obliged to pay several dollars additional in the course of a year for the present mismanaged and utterly unreliable service?

No Difference. There is no difference, except in degree, in the public highway, the surface car-line, the elevated road above, or the subway route beneath. All are means of travel and transportation for the general public. All are arteries of the social body, and, by the same token, all ought to be used without reservation by the general public, and paid for — so long as capitalism lasts — out of the common people's treasury. Any other solution of the transportation problem would be temporary and not permanent. This being obliged to stop to make change, deposit a fare in a box, or purchase a ticket to be taken up by a conductor, before starting on a car ride, is stupid to the point of ennui. It has nothing whatever to do with transportation — the thing for which you board a car — and should not be tolerated any longer by sensible people. The same is true of the postal system. All of our mail ought to be transported without direct charge, and the costs of such service met by still further taxation if necessary.

The Result

The time is fast approaching, if it has not already arrived, when the mere cost of "doing business" is greater than the system will bear. Therefore, "production for use" must shortly supplant the present "production for profit."

Today the highest wages are paid not for creating and producing, but for selling and advertising! This is a curious anomaly which grows ever more anomalous. There is no limit to the salary of the successful salesman, while the wages of the mechanic, farmer, clerk and laborer are limited by the law of supply and demand or fixed unalterably by the omnipresent labor union. Such a condition of affairs cannot be healthy and conducive to fair dealing. Resentment and misunderstanding cannot but ensue from so one-sided an arrangement. Business, in one form or another, has enslaved us all.

The cost of doing business today is often one-third of the retail price of most commodities. This is not as it should be. People cannot continue to pay a third of their incomes for frills and service instead of for sustenance. Given unrestricted scope, unhampered by war, the modern methods of merchandising would have soon dragged themselves down in one great cataclysm. Fortunately (or unfortunately, as the case may be) the unseen hand of fate turned loose the most destructive war in history. From the hour when the present war struck, other forces than those of industrial evolution took up the task of making the world safe for Democracy. The forces now at work to bring safety and security upon the earth can be trusted to see to it that the modern Moloch of "business" shall not devour the lives of earth's people in the same measure as before the present war.

The Present Paradox

Nothing could be more inane and childish than our utter dependence on the capitalist idea of doing business. To visionless souls nothing is possible unless you have the capital in hand with which to initiate an enterprise. "How are you going to pay for all this?" is the question they inevitably ask. The answer, again, is simplicity itself:

Millions of human beings engaged in useless forms of employment; other millions engaged in doing nothing at all; millions of lazy, shiftless individuals who don't want to work because they are unable to live decently on the pitifully small wage their labor will bring in the present market; millions who want work and can't get it (in normal times of peace) — and all the while society is rotting and festering with poverty and the fruits of mismanagement!

Private capital can't see any return in employing people who are out of work unless there is a favorable market for their product. Private capital cannot be persuaded to venture into many enterprises which are sorely in need of development in the interest of the common weal. Private capital, taken all in all, is insufficient anyway when one pauses to reflect on the number and variety of things which society is clamoring to accomplish and which really need doing in the interest of human progress.

PRESENT SYSTEM ILLOGICAL

How can people whose wages are periodically cut off by the recurrent breakdowns of privately managed enterprise purchase sufficient goods to enable private business to resume operation in order that they may again receive their customary wages? Here is the paradox of privately owned capitalistic enterprise. Such a system no longer serves society. It has become worn out and archaic.

Soon some other — more intelligent and

better adapted system of public enterprise —
must intervene to save the situation. It is intolerable to think of our ever reverting to the
status quo ante bellum when peace finally arrives.
Such a system has been "weighed in the balance and found wanting" for a generation.

A New System Called For. In place of capitalistic incompetence and the sheer inability of
private enterprise to meet the demands of the
new day, why not attempt such a solution of
the problem as will endure so long as society
itself shall last?

That one industry should pay a higher wage
than another for the same quality of effort is
unqualifiedly wrong and unjust. Since so many
palpable injustices exist under the present
system — injustices which are an intrinsic part
of the system and which can never be gotten
rid of so long as the present system endures —
isn't it far wiser to change the system than to
hobble along, dragging such a dead weight of
injustice and unfitness? Why prune the
branches when the trouble is with the root?

CHAPTER III

OBJECTIONS MET

Why not take human nature into account and initiate a plan whereby society will be secured against a repetition of the present holocaust?

Human Nature. "Human nature wants all it can get," you declare. Exactly. Therefore, why not so organize our way of doing things that this particular streak in human nature will find fullest gratification? Unstinted production of all kinds of commodities is the surest and quickest way to give greedy human nature its fill of every bodily requirement.

Why should the few have their human nature gratified to the utmost, while the many look on in envy and seek to rob and cajole the few into parting with some of their over-abundant substance? Is envy a good thing to breed in the hearts of men? Does society exist for the cultivation of the baser motives in men? Why not,

by a rational ordering of social processes, do
away with that which cankers and corrodes
the souls of both rich and poor under our crazy-
quilt system now in operation?

WHY GREEDY?

"Human nature" is the result of the fact
that, until now, there has never been enough of
this world's goods to go around. In a state of
nature the very hardness of the struggle for
enough to eat — to say nothing of the struggle
for trinkets and objects of possession — permitted only the survival of the strongest. The
desire to gobble up everything in sight results
from the age-old insufficiency of bodily comforts. Nature was formerly meagre with her
gifts. The world was lean, and there was never
enough of anything to suffice. Hence the crafti-
est and the strongest secured what there was,
and the remainder gradually became enslaved
by those who became the possessors.

All this is readily understood after a moment's reflection. The human nature which we
have inherited is innately jealous of anything
which would deprive us of sufficient food, clothing and shelter. But, remember, this instinct
(call it the instinct of self-preservation if you
will) is the outcome of ages of economic insufficiency wherein the food supply was perennially uncertain and meagre.

Do we not forget that we are living in an age of scientific production and distribution? Are we not prone to lose sight of the fact that — barring war — there is no danger of the world's food supply ever becoming short again?

Times have changed. Human nature manifests itself differently under different environments. With fifty hungry men all seeking a single baked potato, human nature expresses itself in a different manner than in the case of the same number of men beholding a sumptuous banquet table laden with all manner of food in abundance. Yet the presence of one condition as contrasted with the other hasn't changed human nature one whit. Society should seek to acquaint itself with human nature and thereby avoid things which provoke the worst in men.

"Selfishness" Eliminated. Under the programme of unlimited production which would result from the operation of the plan indicated there would be no desire on the part of anyone to undo his neighbor. When all are assured of enough and to spare, then — and not until then — will that which is best in human nature find expression. People don't make hogs of themselves in the presence of variety and abundance so long as they are assured that there is plenty more where that which they are enjoying came from.

In these days of wholesale production there is no good reason why any one should go poorly or shabbily dressed. Under the régime which must eventually be adopted every one will enjoy the ability to dress becomingly and to express his personality to its fullest — a privilege which is at present possible only to the fortunate few. Can any one doubt the desirability of such a wholesome state of affairs? Yet how many poverty-pinched souls today live drab and colorless lives for want of the necessary money to exercise their legitimate tastes in matters of dress and adornment.

In the Matter of Dress

Does it serve society for men and women to be kept forever conscious of their inability to appear to advantage in the presence of others? How is progress effected by undermining an individual's self-respect? What an abundance of individuality and originality would be liberated by the simple process of allowing every one to help himself from the common stores of a humane and beneficent social order! It requires but slight imagination to picture the thousand and one benefits which would be opened to all by the functioning of such a programme.

Present Rate of Progress. So long as we depend on the initiative of private capital, little widespread progress will henceforth be made. The very niggardliness of all forms of capitalism prevent it from serving a great while longer. What a paradox for miners to freeze because they have mined more coal than people have the money to purchase, or for tailors to go in rags because they have made too many suits of clothes? The collective common sense of men and women must, it would seem, soon put an end to such stupidity.

Millions of people want more of life's good things. Millions more could use to advantage ten times what they are now permitted to enjoy. Yet, as often happens under capitalism, millions are homeless and without food. Other millions are freezing and starving for lack of fuel and adequate nourishment.

PRESENT-DAY BLINDNESS

What wise man or woman would sit idly by and starve with food almost within grasp, and not exert himself? But this is precisely what a large percentage of the people are doing from year to year in all so-called civilized countries in times of peace! What blindness — what vapidity — for people to exist in such a fashion. Words fail to express the inanity of it. Is the present social order the best that educated brains and trained leadership can give us? If so — then away with such brains and leadership! We will henceforth have none of them!

People need goods of every kind in order to live abundantly. Many forms of work relating to public improvements are crying to be done. The development of the nation's water powers, for example, is urgently needed to supply the country with heat, light and power. Yet private capital cannot be shown a sufficient profit incentive to venture along many much-needed lines. Is the nation going to stand still and idly wait for some good fairy to accomplish what every one agrees is for the common good? Are we to do without many of the improvements and advantages which by universal consent are deemed to be for the health and welfare of human life, but which private capital finds no profit in producing? It were incredible that such a state of affairs could continue to exist among intelligent human beings.

NECESSARY PUBLIC WORKS

Why cannot society offer employment on needed public works to every person not necessary to the production of commodities, and see to it that sufficient abundance of economic wealth is produced so that both the immediate producer and he who labors for the remote benefit of society shall find no dearth of worldly rewards? Such a plan ought not to be difficult for brains which can build the Panama Canal.

The moment human labor is applied to anything results begin to appear. All the machinery necessary to the foundation of unstinted production is now in existence. Already — in the absence of war — there is available the complete physical equipment of such a plan as is here advocated. It is not as if the race were to begin all over again. That is not the proposition.

Simply to keep on as we are, but with the abolition of every kind of non-productive employment and the absence of future payment of any sort — this is the gist of the proposition. And it is feasible if men will only have the courage to attempt it. I believe it can and will be done.

Unlimited Production Possible. Modern machine processes, scientific discoveries and labor-saving devices have increased man's productive capacity a thousand fold. Under our modern division of labor every worker produces proportionately several times the value of what he is permitted to enjoy. With an even less number of hours than the conventional eight-hour day, half of the population, if given a free rein, could produce enough and to spare for the entire one hundred per cent.

This would enable at least a third of the people now alive to be engaged on useful public works. Their maintenance would come from the enormous surplus produced by the remainder of the population engaged in the production of consumable wealth. There are no catches in this. It is "as plain as daylight." All that is required to make it practical is the courage to attempt it and the belief that it can be done.

DESIRES FULFILLED

Everybody wants to live. Everybody wants to play. Millionaires live and play. The birds, animals and fishes live and play. The creator placed no artificial barriers in the way of the lower animals' right to "life, liberty and the pursuit of happiness." Man is the only animal which denies himself the right to live and play. What consummate folly to live without living! Yet more than eighty per cent of mankind do just that and nothing else! Isn't it about time men learned how to live? Isn't it nearly time mankind received some benefit from the invention, toil and struggle of the ages? What a Frankenstein society has become to the vast majority of the people whose brain and brawn are welded into its very vitals. How insensate for men to be trampled underfoot and ground to powder by the very object of their own creation! The car of Juggernaut still rides roughshod over the bodies and souls of a majority of earth's suffering millions.

More Anomalies

Today the biggest wasters are considered the country's chief asset. The wealthy man or woman who buys the most clothes, food, automobiles, houses, ships, jewelry, is lauded and applauded by every one who has anything to sell. The business community spends thousands of dollars annually trying to entice people to purchase what they do not want and to discard that which they already have.

All modern business is run by and for the people who have money to spend. The man who has nothing to spend receives no consideration from any one. It may be no fault of his. He may have been thrown out of his employment by over industry. Perhaps he worked himself out of a job (as regularly happens in peace times under the existing way of doing things).

At all events, unless one is prepared to consume more than he needs and has the money to pay for it — he is not a desirable customer. Many so-called "specialty shops" exist simply as a monument to the foibles and extravagance of the privileged classes. The customer who spends most lavishly is catered to from the moment his limousine touches the curb. Store flunkies have orders to "be nice" to certain customers because they are prodigious wasters of things into which other people have put their very heart's blood.

Social Enemies. In the matter of personal selfishness the well-to-do who surround themselves with servants and flunkies are among society's worst enemies. Instead of "giving employment" to the vast army of worthies of both sexes who are engaged in all forms of "personal service," these purblind rich are condemning millions of people to labor in field and mart and factory a longer time than necessary to produce what society needs.

SELFISH WASTE

Every individual enticed from the economic field means one less producer to do the world's work. So the millions of people who minister to the whims and idiosyncracies of the well-to-do, thereby become an added burden on the backs of the producers and help to increase the length of the work-day for those who shoulder the real burdens of society. The popular superstition that "the rich" are society's true benefactors because they "furnish jobs" to the poor man is forever discredited. Under capitalism the well-to-do are society's worst enemies. They not only produce nothing themselves, but they prevent others from producing anything by offering them flattering wages to cater to their selfish whims and foibles. Does any one suppose for a moment that such a condition will be tolerated when society is once aroused to the enormity of such social crimes?

Present-day society is one long, living lie. Sham, pretence, show, vanity, envy, jealousy and several other of the meaner attributes of our much-maligned "human nature" compose its chief characteristics. Suicides, homicides, robberies and abortions attest to its innate rottenness and brazen injustices. A society in which a single individual finds nothing worth living for stands condemned at the bar of reason *ipse facto*.

More Paradoxes

Not the least of the ironical aspects of our present social madness lies in the effort being made to induce people to save — while ten thousand voices in every window, street car and daily newspaper cry, "Spend, spend, spend." "The Society for the Encouragement of American Thrift" will one day take its place in the archives of American humor along with the writings of Josh Billings, Mark Twain and Artemus Ward.

Any state of society in which waste is at a premium and economy is denounced as niggardly and "un-American" ought not to have a single apologist or champion. Yet there are comparatively few who are bold enough to denounce the present order for what they know in their hearts it has actually become.

CHAPTER IV

PENALTIES

By Their Fruits Ye Shall Know Them

If society is known by its fruits, who can sincerely avow himself in favor of a continuance of the existing social order? Things have arrived at such a point that whoever stands squarely for a continuance of things as they are is exceedingly likely to find himself in bad company. Kaiser Wilhelm is undoubtedly the shining product and leading exponent of the ancient and honorable order of world-grabbers. Potsdam is the logical output of "whatever is, is right."

When the proposal is made to abolish all currency, payments and mediums of exchange in the interest of world happiness and eternal good-will, there immediately arise a host of vociferous objectors. They cannot rightly be designated as "conscientious objectors" for their adherence to the present order of things brands them as already conscienceless. "Noisy objectors" one particularly strenuous objector might characterize them.

Another Objection. "If everybody were permitted to consume all he wanted out of the joint production of society, the few would have things all their own way, and the most selfish would predominate as at present," I hear some one object.

Ah, but you forget that a man can wear only one suit of clothes at a time, and that everybody must do some useful work in order to avoid being locked up under the proposed scheme of things. Isn't it true that the best way to teach people that too much candy is not good for them is to allow them to have all the sweets they can devour? The temporary intoxication which would be likely to result from allowing people to partake of as much as they could legitimately consume, would soon be offset by a sane, well-regulated middle course. There is nothing like excess to teach people the wisdom of a happy medium in anything.

NATURE'S PENALTY

Nature penalizes overindulgence just as certainly as day follows night. "No man can wrong the universe," said Emerson. The animals and birds which have survived the rigors of nature for a million generations or more

need no artificial restraint to teach them how
to enjoy nature's provisions for their welfare
and happiness. Although civilization has largely
deprived us of our instincts, it would seem a
reasonable proposition that men still have
sense enough to regulate their conscious existence on a scale at least as rational as that
followed by the humbler inhabitants of the
earth.

When people realize that, no matter how
much they may consume, there will never again
be a dearth of the things upon which humanity
depends for its existence, they will not want
to gorge themselves with the fruits of production. There is nothing like a surfeit of anything
to induce a wholesome disregard of the future.
Men become parsimonious and hoard things
only when they fear that there is likelihood of
their not being able to get any more of a particular commodity.

Assure the people of the world that never
again will they be in want so long as everybody
contributes to the general welfare of society by
a well-regulated amount of daily toil, and
never again will men crowd and push at the
table of life. This aspect of human nature is
just as innate in men as its opposite. Environment is everything. Circumstances alter cases.

Instead of provoking the worst in human
nature — which the present social order (dis-

order) tends to do — the programme here
advocated would speedily draw out the latent
humanity in all men and provide the foundation
for the "Kingdom of God" on earth. Men are
not God-like while struggling in a free-for-all
fight for their daily bread. Present conditions
are a systematic denial of the right of every
man to moral and spiritual growth.

The safest way to protect the common welfare under the changed form of society which
this plan would interpose would be to permit
every one to help himself — without money and
without price — to the joint product of humanity.

COMMUNITY OF INTEREST

Then, the individual would have no incentive
to grab for himself more than he could use. A
surplus would do him no good, for he couldn't
sell it. Every one would have access to the
common stores — properly supervised of course
— and would neither desire nor covet anything
which his neighbor might possess.

All incentive to steal or plunder would be
automatically taken away. If an individual
saw anything he wanted which another had,
he could get a duplicate of it — whether collar
button or limousine — in short order. Where
would be the so-called "crimes against prop-
erty" under such a system? It is safe to predict

that nine-tenths of the crimes against the person which now result from arguments and brawls over money or possessions would likewise be eliminated by the new order.

TEMPTATION MINIMIZED

Lawyers and their satellites, agents, salesmen, advertising employees, bankers, brokers, business experts and their host of paid retainers, would find themselves in better business under the changed state. No longer would temptation stalk abroad in every bank and office. Never again would weak humanity be penalized by arbitrary fines and jail terms for not possessing the moral stamina to withstand temptation.

Restraint. No one supposes for a moment that all restraint could be immediately done away with under the suggested programme. Jails and places of discipline would still exist for a while. The difference, however, between the jails of the future and those of today would be in the number and character of their inmates.

Crime. Instead of shutting men and women up for stealing, as at present, the real malefactors in the coming order of society would be all those who wasted the common substance of the State. The reckless and unrestrained use of that into which men have put their sweat and labor would become the real crime against society. Provision might be made for jailing for a reasonable period any one who was proved to have taken from the general wealth of production more than he could honestly make use of.

The Biggest Criminal. Waste and extravagance would be "high crimes and misdemeanors" under the new social order. Laziness and indolence would likewise be stigmatized as "felonies." "He who steals my purse steals trash" would become the literal truth in the days that are ahead. That which would injure society most, as then constituted, would be any form of endeavor which was calculated to evade rendering service to society. Not to serve in the general scheme of things would be the blackest of crimes. Parisitism, or attempted parisitism, would be punishable with long terms of social ostracism. Perhaps, instead of jails and prisons, those who attempted to defraud society would be compelled to wear a placard branding them for what they are — despoilers of the common good! How different all this sounds as compared with the rank injustices and social blindness of today!

Nature's Way. Because of the penalty which Nature inexorably imposes on those who violate her all-wise laws of health and efficiency, enlightened humanity could more and more dispense with restraint as a punishment, until

finally Nature could be trusted to impose all
the punishment necessary.

RIDICULE EFFECTIVE

The extraordinary girth resulting from overindulgence in eating; the bloated features,
bleary eyes and stupid expression which come
from habitual gormandizing, would be their
own badges of demerit imposed by an all-wise
Providence. When such ear-marks of selfishness and unwise indulgence are no longer in
good taste with the majority of society,
Nature's own branding iron can be trusted to
fulfill all the demands of decency and justice.
Such an offender would be viewed with loathing
by all good citizens. No other punishment
could be one-half as severe.

Deprivation. In the matter of crime and
punishment — what more effective method of
correction would be needed than to withhold
for a time the right of the offending individual
to partake of the bounty of society? Those
who wouldn't co-operate intelligently, and
who persisted in loafing or wasting, could be
more effectively dealt with by depriving them
of access to social benefits than by any other
means. To compel the offending man or woman
to go without new clothes, hats, shoes or
amusements would be punishment indeed in a
society where no one was compelled except

from choice to wear old clothes and do without recognized and approved forms of social entertainment.

Police. How would the person who offended against the common weal be detected in such a free-for-all social system? If no police were necessary, and no account of goods taken or consumed was kept, how would it be known that any one was hoarding, wasting or idling? The answer rests in the well-known fact of human nature again. Where all have an interest in the State, and consciously participate in the social system, it follows that every one is a proprietor or participator in the common product of such a system.

IDENTITY OF INTEREST

When your interest and mine are identical, we would both be quick to feel the injustice of either of us defrauding the other. So, under such a system as has been here forcasted any one who takes more than he needs steals from all, and all would be on the lookout to see that no one took more than he could legitimately use.

Every case of attempted hoarding, extravagance or non-contributory idleness would be immediately reported to some designated tribunal which would, after trying the complaint, impose the well-merited punishment.

Under such a system children would be taught from the cradle that waste, extravagance and laziness were the cardinal sins against society, and would be keen to observe any infraction of social principles.

Espionage. Every individual would be on the lookout to see that no one defrauded him — even as is the case today — (that is human nature) and, under the new order, would be quick to report any and all cases where individuals were even suspected of not doing their share of, or squandering the joint product of, social effort. No other system of surveillance or espionage would be called for. Enlightened self-interest would be quite sufficient to guarantee against continued violation on the part of an offender. In fact, the inclination to defraud the common weal would soon disappear under such a system. When the benefits of such a way of living are fully realized, few indeed would be the individuals who would seek to evade responsibility. Under our present form of society the evasion of responsibility is constant and flagrant.

CHAPTER V

CHARACTER AND IDEALS

Character. Who is there so bold as to claim that our present iniquitous social system produces the highest or finest types of character? Rarely, if ever, are the so-called successful men of the present day to be envied in any trait of character they possess. People envy them their ability to make money, but those who really desire to acquire the ordinary habits of mind which go with money-making are few and far between. Instead, how many pure-hearted, honest, simple-minded and genuine spirits are content to occupy humble positions and go without many bodily comforts rather than sell their souls' wealth for mere pottage! It is the everlasting paradox of the present order that "virtue is its own reward." Such an admission brands the existing order as bestial, faulty, and in violation of all sound ethical and moral principles.

Ideals. Who in all seriousness can speak a

good word for the maintenance of a social order in which every youth and maiden must part company with his or her ideals upon reaching maturity? How can any one justify the continuance of a world in which disillusionment is the saddest tragedy in the life of every one who grows up? What hypocrisy to teach children the conventional morality only to have them turn on their teachers with reproach when they discover the underlying truth of existence today to be the dog-eat-dog struggle of antiquity!

Reason. What justification can be found in reason for the perpetuation of a social system where only the strong are wanted, and where the richest rewards go to those who contribute the least to human welfare? What right to endure has the present order in which daily several hundred people are murdered and as many more — unable to cope with the unequal struggle — take their own lives in order to be out of it all? Who of any intelligence believes that it is a good thing to drive people to desperation by injustice and temptation, and then merely pity such victims of environment because they were unable to stand the strain?

Efficiency. What kind of a system is it that demands a type of efficiency which is altogether extraordinary, and denies to all who do not happen to be born with the required amount of energy, a place in the sun? Is it not true that our present way of living and doing business is adapted only to a race of super-men and women who do not really exist? Does not this account for the appalling number of suicides, failures and "unfits" which can all be laid at the door of this hellish way of living? Is it any wonder that some of our best and bravest men and women believe that the world is going to the dogs?

Callousness. It is not expected that so-called successful people who have been made hard and callous by virtue of their success will answer these questions in favor of a more humanitarian way of living. "Every one can do what I have done" is no answer at all. It is just possible that those who answer in that fashion are blinded by their success to the fact that few people are sufficiently anxious to be reckoned as successful, if to be successful means to be like the ordinary exponent of commercial success today!

AMBITION: INCENTIVE

There will be a goodly number of honest individuals who will object to the thesis here maintained on the ground that such a system of capital-less production and distribution would provide no opportunity for the legitimate development of ambition. "What of ambi-

tion?" they say; "where do you find opportunity for men to grow and expand under your
system?"

Again I offer "human nature" as the true
basis of ambition.

If by ambition our critic means the unrestricted desire to make money — to "get
rich" at the expense of others — then I must
admit that such a trait has no place in the coming order. The desire to make money and to
build up a great commercial or financial enterprise is inherent only in a form of society where
money is the all-important factor, as under
capitalism. But I presuppose the utter and
complete abolition of any medium of exchange
whatsoever. Hence, where there is no such a
thing as money, there can be no desire to
"make money" or to become "financially inde-
pendent." The proposition is to put temptation along that line out of men's way, as
catering only to the baser motives in men.

Distinguished from Greed. Ambition which
pauperizes others is not ambition in any true
sense. It is only inhuman greed. That is a trait
in our animal nature which needs to be gotten
rid of. One of the chief virtues of the coming
society is the fact that it contains no realm in
which the desire of unworthy men to "lord
it over" their brothers can find expression. If
those desires still remain it will be considered

doing the possessor of such "ambitions" a favor to put him behind bars where he can no longer injure and defraud the common good. If further answer to such criticism is called for it can be found in the fact that the only opportunity for ambition to find expression in the new society will be in creation and administration.

Service. Every laudable ambition will find gratification in the endeavor to serve society nobly and well. Since no one will desire money, and since there will be no place at which money can be spent, ambition to power and affluence through accumulation will be eliminated. Only in a state of barbarism like the present is money coveted. When all are joint shareholders in the corporation of society, all will share alike in the benefits (not "earnings") of the corporation. And since an abundance of every worthwhile commodity will be available for the mere asking, no one will have any incentive to either accumulate or defraud.

A Salutary System

Such a state of affairs, by eliminating the opportunity to enrich oneself at the expense of others, will save the would-be oppressor from himself. Only laudable ambition would consequently find a place in the new order of society. When stocks and bonds, interest, rents and dividends, with their inevitable injustices, are forever eliminated, all possibility of accumulation and money-power will be precluded.

At present the number of people who want to do business is altogether out of proportion to the amount of business which needs to be done. Figures state that ninety per cent of all business ventures wind up in the bankruptcy courts. The loss to society from this source is something fearful. Already the number of people who are in business for the sole purpose of making money is wholly disproportionate to the quantity and quality of the service rendered to society. So common has mere money-making, as distinguished from real service, become, that the customary salutation of men meeting on the street is not "What are you doing for a living now?" but rather, "What's your graft these days?"

Today's Failure. Today, as business is run, there is not sufficient legitimate business to go around. By that it is meant that the inadequacy of our existing form of endeavor to provide a place for all those who wish to do business is woefully apparent. Because there is not enough honest business to satisfy the craving of all who desire to do business, thousands take to the business of debauching their fellow men. The liquor, drug, gambling and white-slave businesses are living witnesses to this truth. Failure to find a profitable place in the existing scheme of things leads those of "business instincts" to commercialize all the foibles and weaknesses of their fellow men. "How are the mighty fallen."

Our civilization has grown to be a government by "business," and almost no other voice except that of organized labor is heard in our halls of legislation.

Business and the State

So great have profits become under our present business arrangements that corporations and "trusts" are able, out of their "earnings," to lend their employees for what should be purely governmental functions. Many things deemed to be of a public or semi-public nature are "put through" by certain wealthy corporations without expense to the people. Yet the people pay the bills indirectly through the excessive prices they pay for the commodity put forth by the particular corporation in question. Thus the corporations have assumed a *quasi* public character and have arrogated to themselves the sovereign right of states to levy taxes upon the people.

"Invisible" Government. Time was when business earned only a comfortable living for its proprietors. But business has been subject to the laws of growth and change to the same

extent as other social institutions. All are
amenable to the Divine urge we naïvely term
Evolution.

"Invisible government" has become a fact
which no intelligent man or woman can afford
to ignore. Rare is the representative of the
people who is able to perennially withstand the
promptings of our modern "money power."
Nothing short of the elimination of money —
the *modus operandi* of these forces — will return
the control of the State and of the forces of
production to the hands of the democratic
people of the earth.

Recreation. The objection that the operation
of this new system would be conducive to
weakness and flaccidity of character is not well
taken. For people to get their work done in
the morning and then to hurry off to golf links,
beach or trotting park does not necessarily
indicate a lack of stamina and poise. For
people to work interminably without recreation or diversion is the height of folly, as any
physician will tell you. The man or woman
who does not take some recreation, even under
our present system, is foredoomed to atrophy
and death before his time. Recreation is the
modern safety valve. Without it normality
would perish.

Dulling Monotony. For men to work like
Trojans at soul-stifling and sense-benumbing

occupations leads only to mental, moral and spiritual perversion. Because life has become so mechanical and intense, it is good to have frequent and prolonged relaxation in order to recoup the dissipated energies of mankind. We live so much at fever heat that men need the relief which recreation affords. The "fittest" men under our present system are those men who have not forgotten how to play. The man or woman who has ceased to play has literally ceased to live in any true measure.

PLAY AND TRAVEL

Everybody wants to enjoy life; everybody wants to travel and see things; everybody wants recreation and diversion at times. But comparatively few people under the existing scheme of things really live at all. Drudgery is the common and inescapable lot of the vast majority of mankind. Even those who become "successful" do so in the majority of instances at the expense of health, character and refinement.

It doesn't break the morale of the businessman to play golf, hunt, yacht or motor in his spare time. Rather is his value and ability increased by such diversions. What reason is there to suppose that playtime would not be profitably used if it were to be had by every mechanic, office grind and machine operative in existence? The lack of such opportunity puts more people in their graves than the abuse of it.

Pleasures. If things come with comparative ease, as they are bound to do under the new society, what is to prevent all people from making use of the exclusive pleasures now possible only to the well-to-do? Society would be not poorer, but richer, from such a course. So long as all adults are obliged to contribute the maximum amount of work required for social production, no one ever need fear that the stamina of the workers would be undermined. What undermines character and weakens the morale of men is long hours, low wages, bad environment and unrequited toil.

Diseases of Character

What blasts characters, undermines morality, breeds laziness and weakens social restraint is getting something for nothing, as under the present social system. The receipt of unearned increment, dividends on watered stock, excessive profit, rents, interest and rebates,— these are the real enemies to character development. So long as some people receive that which they have not earned, others must continue to earn that which they do not get. This is irrefutable. The one thing which undermines the morale of the individual more than any other is striving to live without working. To attempt to live by one's wits and to render no socially valuable equivalent for that which one receives from society is the chief cause of moral laxity and distorted views of life. Trying to secure something for nothing — as in the case of stock gambling — is the damnation of morals and character alike. But this is what *capitalism* offers — not the rational society of the future.

CHAPTER VI

LABOR AND LEISURE

The Dignity of Labor. One very transparent
benefit which would immediately result from
the new order would be that labor would be
restored to a position of dignity and honor,
now merely a polite fiction of campaign orators.
Owing to the age-old desire of certain people
to avoid work by working the workers, we
have arrived at a stage where the artisan who
works with his hands and brain eight or ten
hours a day is considered the legitimate spoil
of the clever ones who live alone by their wits.

Because the benefits which have been conferred upon humanity by the invention of
labor-saving machinery have been monopolized
by the few, and used for the purpose of creating "income" instead of happiness, manual
and mental toil is still low-paid drudgery,
something to be avoided if possible and done
only under protest at all. The place of the
creator of the world's real wealth is not an

enviable one after centuries of struggle and achievement.

Wage Slavery. Physical labor — under the wage system — is still another form of slavery, and everybody who can escape from it does so with no regrets. Labor is today, as always, monotonous, dulling, soul-destroying, because of its sordid, unchanging grind. Labor for no longer a period than might be necessary to provide the coming age with whatever men desire, will become wholesome exercise.

Instead of manual labor being the blessing that it was evidently intended to be, it has been made well-nigh despised among men. Almost every father who is engaged in bringing up a family of children frankly says, "I want to give my children an education so that they will not have to struggle along as I have done."

Real Labor Despised. Young people of both sexes are brought up to expect jobs which require them to be dressed up in a white collar and necktie, or a silk waist and dress skirt, as the case may be. Few if any young people ever expect to live by the sweat of their brows or the toil of their hands. Mothers and fathers everywhere "want their children to be freed from the manual struggle" and to be "fine gentlemen" and "fine ladies," as far as possible. Real labor is everywhere to be avoided, and sorry indeed is the lot of the boy or girl who hasn't the "gumption" to escape from useful toil as a means of livelihood.

Rome's Downfall. Do we need the warning which presaged the downfall of Rome to awaken us to the seriousness of such a situation? No nation is safe in which the "dignity of labor" is not respected and encouraged. Honest toil should be the first badge of culture. No accomplishment, however able, can wholly compensate for a lack of decent participation in the fundamental work of the world.

The Joy of Creation

All normal individuals like to do things with their hands. No greater joy exists than beholding material things grow into useful articles under skilful manipulation. The trouble with society is that some have appropriated all the benefits and leisure which machinery has conferred upon mankind, while other men have been "permitted" to use the machines only on consideration that they give four-fifths of their product to the machine owner. Our present industrial chaos is the result.

Under the new order all able-bodied men and women — not engaged in the nurture of children — will delight to work a few hours a day if they are made to realize that it is their labor which produces enough and to spare for themselves and their dependents indiscriminately.

People do not mind working if they know that
what they produce belongs to themselves and
those they love. What makes present-day
labor a thing to be avoided is the fact that no
man is allowed to work on a machine, or in
any other capacity, unless he suffers himself to
be defrauded of a portion of his product by the
one who provided the machine or opportunity
for labor.

The Love of Work. When men are allowed to
work as by divine right, and no parasites are
allowed to squander and gamble with the fruits
of honest toil, then, and not until then,
will labor come into its own. The machinery
of society is the legacy of the ages — rightfully
considered — and should no more be used by
the fortunate few to enslave the many, than
the land should be used, as it is today, for the
same purpose.

The alleged argument that men would deteriorate under such a system I have no sympathy
with. Men are literally rotting their lives away
today. Don't forget that. Who is so inane as
to suppose that an individual is going to become "lazy, indolent and untractable" if
convinced that he is receiving his whole product
for the first time since the departure of men
from primitive industrial methods?

Millions of people would enjoy working a few
hours a day, if assured that their very livelihood

depended upon it and that it would bring them the fruits which they have a right to expect, where those same people will not work at all today because they know that they are being exploited, and that knowledge takes away their natural incentive to work for a living.

No one can gainsay that the tendency today on the part of those successful individuals who have reached the top of the ladder is to deteriorate mentally, morally and physically. One need but survey a gathering of the much-lauded "successful business men" to be impressed with the tendency of modern capitalism and competition to annihilate body, mind and soul. If our modern "captains of industry" are types, may God have mercy on the race under uninterrupted competition.

Health. Does any one question for an instant the assertion that such men as are representative of modern plutocracy would be healthier and more efficient mentally, morally, physically and spiritually if compelled to labor a few hours a day at real manual toil in place of their present occupations?

Modern competition makes neither for health or longevity. The well-known "diseases of middle life" which kill so many prematurely today, are the result of the one-sided, narrow, competitive living demanded in many cases as a price for commercial success under the present system. No sooner does the average man become successful today than he begins to deteriorate as a result of his success. Once freed from the necessity of struggling because of the accumulation of a fortune, inhibition and atrophy — often coupled with excess of eating, drinking and so-called pleasure — set in, and the end results prematurely in thousands of instances. As many people die because of "prosperity" as from the lack of it.

Joy of Living. Nothing but a well-regulated, joyous, productive existence — which would be demanded by the operation of the new order — is worthy of intelligent and aspiring men and women. And the new order would demand and secure just that. It is the duty of society to save men from themselves. A moderate amount of daily toil would take the place of more violent exercise, and fully compensate in man's development for the lack of locomotion resulting from our modern recourse to many and varied forms of transportation.

Proof. Statistics prove that the clergy, who often combine manual labor of their own choosing with "plain living and high thinking," live the longest of any class of individuals. The clergy as a class are as fecund as any group of their size in society, and their progeny rise to higher places on an average than do the other classes in State and Nation. Which only goes to prove that a well-regulated, reflective, self-controlled existence in which both body and soul have room to expand is the best possible state for mortal man to enjoy.

Deserved Leisure. Sociologists tell us that learning and culture had their origin in the valley of the Nile because there, of all places on the earth, it was easier to live. The Nile valley is the most fertile and productive of any locality in the world. Therefore the ancients found it easier to combat the forces of nature. Because the means of life were realized with small expenditure of human effort, men were enabled to evolve language, art and literature, while their less-favored brethren scattered over the world were kept busy struggling with nature in the endeavor to secure the bare necessities of life. By conferring an abundant leisure which resulted from a minimum expenditure of effort, Nature made it possible for men to expand mentally and spiritually. Leisure is a prerequisite to intellectual and spiritual development and expansion.

ART AND LITERATURE

All of the mediæval works of art, sculpture, music and literature were done either under the patronage of kings or of the church. Never do men expand to their fullest when held down by soul-destroying toil. Especially is this true of

our modern high-speed machine processes
which call for dead uniformity of operation.
The very automatic character of much of our
modern machinery is horribly monotonous.
No wonder machine "hands" seek the saloon
and other forms of questionable relaxation to
brighten and bolster up their jaded spirits after
a day's work. Modern machine labor lacks
most of the painstaking originality which was
demanded in the "elder days of art" where
builders "wrought with greatest care." Since
the disappearance of hand methods of production labor has lost much, if not all, of its native
charm and creative virtue. Hence the need of
more abundant leisure than heretofore in which
the increasing number of machine-tenders may
rehabilitate themselves.

Shallow Thinking. Those who raise the objection to the proposed plan that it provides
no room for the proper exercise of legitimate
pride of creation and organization, simply
haven't thought the thing through. Every fair-
minded individual will admit without hesita-
tion that, so far as a well-rounded existence
goes, society could well dispense with all further
inventions and improvements of any sort. If
no further inventions or devices were to be
discovered throughout all time there would be
no lack of variety or abundance of economic
goods. In other words, the mind and hand of

man have perfected sufficient industrial equipment and processes to provide for every legitimate human want for the next one thousand years, at the very least.

All that remains necessary is to multiply those mechanical and industrial marvels now existing to secure adequate supplies of all desirable commodities for an indefinite period. Yet inventors will never cease their attempts to save labor and increase production. The pity of it is that, with the added emancipation of men and women brought about by machinery, the private ownership of machinery for profit has resulted in emancipating the owners, but *not the operators* of such machinery. Instead of such invention conferring leisure upon all the race, it has thus far only enslaved men the more.

"CREATIVE PRIDE" SLIGHT

With the increase of "machine-made" products, both in the realm of consumption and of art, much, if not all, individual pride of creation has vanished. No longer do the commercial specimens of handicraft bear the trademark of the individual creating them. Production in quantity through a widely distributed division of labor has largely robbed industry of all traces of personality today. Most industrial labor is of the sort which needs doing, but needs little else. Therefore, to get the necessary thing done in the least possible time with the smallest expenditure of energy is the prime consideration. Under such a condition labor is demanded to get out the product, and, with that requirement fulfilled, all interest in the product ceases more often than not.

CHAPTER VII

THE "UNFIT"

The growing burden of the unfit under our decadent capitalistic system constitutes a menace to future growth and development which it would be difficult to overestimate. During the last decade even, the burdens of government — including the caring for that large class of the population which capitalism has thrust below the dead-line of society — rest with added weight upon the so-called normal members of the community.

TAXATION

Taxation of formidable and onerous proportions today crushes the life out of many of those enterprises which the State has licensed to do business. One has but to contemplate the ludicrous efforts of candidates for public office to win votes by promising to reduce the tax rate to obtain evidence of this anomalous condition. The cost of taking care of the injured and wounded who go down in the present unequal struggle for existence continually mounts up.

The standards of modern business are so exacting that millions of the population cannot qualify for paid positions under the existing system. Only the exceptional people are wanted. The ordinary and subnormal folk are compelled to do the dirty work for less than a living wage or become public charges. Thousands prefer to eat the bread of idleness and accept charity from that form of a society which has admitted its responsibility for their inferiority by cheerfully accepting the burden of their support. Present-day society stands convicted of its own stupidity by its recognition of the fact that persons whom society has condemned to inferiority are entitled to sustenance from the common crib.

A Place for All. Under the proposed society of tomorrow all of the "unfit" and economically unemployable people would find their proper niche. Work of various kinds commensurate with their several abilities would be provided for each one, and, instead of being a social burden as they are today, these unfortunate folk would become economically self-supporting. It is unthinkable that such people should ever become adapted to conditions of unrestrained economic competition so long as our present system endures.

Why not provide a society in which every one would find a place and be able to contribute to the common weal? Would not such a system relieve in a large measure the burden of caring for the unfit, and liberate for useful productive or administrative employment millions of officials, guards and caretakers who at present represent a large share of that class of public servants who receive their support from taxation of the rest of the community?

WHY MAKE CRIMINALS?

Today it is certain that people who are unable to adapt themselves to modern business requirements become dependent on charity of one kind or another. Why not, by the simple expediency of sheer volume of production now possible throughout human society, convert this vast liability which capitalism has created and is carrying, into an immediate and valuable social asset? Reason demands that it be done.

Charity. The certainty that an abundance of every commodity would result from such a change as advocated is further indicated by the release of millions of women from the old-fashioned household pursuits labeled "woman's sphere." These liberated modern women who spend their days and nights in so-called "charity work," "relief" and "friendly visiting among the poor" would find no place for such activities in the coming state. Millions of social workers scattered over the face of the earth would no longer find a demand for their puny endeavors. Millions of emancipated men and women would then become productive.

"*Rehabilitation.*" In place of doling out alms and "charity" to the defrauded of society, as practiced today, these well-disposed people would be asked to go to work to help increase the supply from which all would then be entitled to take freely and without stint. Instead of trying to "rehabilitate men" so that they can be de-habilitated again by social injustices, these good people, including the clergy, would be asked to minister to the common welfare of mankind by helping to turn out enough commodities so that their weaker brethren would not be in need of their tender ministrations. This would be equivalent to turning off the faucet which causes the downfall of so many, instead of endeavoring to sop up the overflow.

A Sane Solution: Darwin

Which is the more rational, — attempting to make weak men fit to compete in an impossible social system, or attempting to provide such an abundance of this world's goods that such men would no longer need to be chaperoned in the struggle for existence? Darwin and the evolutionists have shown us that the "struggle for existence" and the "survival of the fittest" result only from an unchecked birthrate among species and an accompanying inadequate food supply. Prodigality of life, accompanied by a dearth of food and other material necessities, undoubtedly played an important part in the struggle of men for "life, liberty and the pursuit of happiness." No one desires to discount that plain fact.

But, now that men have mastered creation and, through invention and discovery, have literally "put all things under their feet" in the realm of economic supply, there is no longer any excuse for attempting to preserve outgrown conditions and the things which were necessitated thereby.

"*Destiny.*" Today, for the first time since creation began, men hold the reins of their future destiny. Blind economic forces unknown and misunderstood no longer circumscribe the progress of the race. By the intelligent manipulation of nature's resources men have demonstrated in the great war that they can produce over a period of years, even under capitalism, enough to satisfy the demands of the civil populations of the world, and sufficient to provide for the maintenance of 40,000,000 fighting men engaged in the most gigantic and wasteful of all earthly extravagances — WAR.

Who is there so lacking in faith, in the face of what the world has been doing for the past four years, as to doubt that the same energy, if aimed toward the elimination of poverty and injustice, could firmly establish the foundations of the social order here outlined?

CHAPTER VIII

IMPORTANT CONSIDERATIONS

Insurance. People who do not at first grasp the magnitude of the proposed plan will ask: What of the aged, the widows and orphans? What will happen to those who depend upon their incomes to exist? What will become of insurance — life insurance, fire insurance, burglar insurance, marine insurance and the rest? How about compensation for injured workingmen and their dependents? What provision is made for the insane, the feeble and the incapable under what you call the "new order" ?

The answer to all the foregoing questions is not difficult. What becomes of all such people at present? What does insurance do now? Such people as the "dependent classes," so-called, exist at the expense of the community. All those who are the recipients of "income" likewise subsist at the expense of the community. Every form of unearned wealth which is consumed by the parasitical classes, both

rich and poor, comes out of the great body of
active workers. Capital, by itself, earns nothing — never did.

THE NEW EMPHASIS

By placing the burden of insurance on the
individual, where it ought not to be, society,
even today, is the loser. Gradually we are
learning that the causes of dependence of one
kind or another are social, not individual. In
spite of all of our logic, society pays the bills
of those who fail to insure themselves individu-
ally. To be sure, present-day society attaches
some opprobrium to those who "go on the town,"
and thereby restrains through their pride many
whose natural inclination is to be "improvident." But the point is that whether people
insure themselves or not, they are provided
for after a fashion even today. The "provident"
not only provide for themselves, but for the
"improvident" as well.

Plenty. Under the "new order" the collective effort of society, unrestrained by private
greed as at present, would produce such an
abundance, that *in plenty*, and in plenty
alone, would be our insurance. The sheer
bounty resulting from man's effort would provide
enough so that, no matter who died, or became
aged, or was taken sick, or was injured, those dependent upon his "support" would be amply

provided for out of society's largess. An overabundance of everything, coupled with the ease with which anything lost or destroyed could be replaced, would obviate the necessity or advantage of any form of insurance.

Social Responsibility. Society, as a whole, should, and will, bear the burdens which are incidental to a complex social existence. Already there is recognition of the fact of social responsibility in the growth of the belief in the wisdom and justice of social insurance and non-contributory old age pensions. With the total abolition of all forms of exchange on a money or price basis, the principle would remain, nevertheless, and all unable to render social service of some sort would simply share in the surplus which would necessarily abound. The small army of insurance and charitable experts which today infest society (and exact a goodly toll for their labors) would simply swell the vaster army of producers or conveyors under the coming social system.

Terms. Under the form of society to-be, the words "expensive" and "inexpensive," "precious," "dear," "costly," "cheap," and all terms relating to price and profit would disappear from the vocabulary. A vocabulary of service with new terms and designations for those who proved their worth by service would instead come gradually into being.

Jewelry. None but the silly would care to ornament their bodies with jewelry, which would be had in such profusion that everybody would sicken of the sight of it. Gold, through the abolition of specie, would become a mere metal of industry, like tin, or pewter, or copper. The sense of value which men now attach to so-called "precious metals" would disappear in a few generations. When nobody wants gold any more, its value will become simply that of any other metal of similar ductile and tensile properties.

Women's Dress. In the matter of dress, the jealousy and pride of women especially could be safely trusted to keep the demands for fine raiment within reasonable bounds. Would Mrs. Jones want a particular gown if she knew that Mrs. Smith, her next-door neighbor, could trot out and return with one just like it? The very ease with which members of the "gentler" sex could bedeck themselves, and the fact that variety in "store clothes" would be probably limited to a certain degree, would undoubtedly stimulate home dressmaking in order to secure originality and express taste.

With the arrival of that day we might reasonably expect to see a far more attractive and becoming mode of dress than that invented for commercial reasons by present-day fashion creators and designers. When every woman is permitted to express her personality to the fullest in clothing of her own choosing — whether home or factory made — then will we behold a fairer and more truly feminine sex than present-day society affords.

THE HOUSING PROBLEM

The question of who will occupy different houses under the coming social order will have to be settled gradually when such conditions arise. Everybody lives somewhere even under the present outgrown system. So all would continue to live in the same dwelling-places in which the new order overtook them until the numerous carpenters and other artisans could build more harmonious and sanitary dwellings for all the people in need of them. The immense volume of female labor which would be liberated by the change to the new order would constitute not the least of the human resources from which the coming society would draw its workers.

Transportation. With regard to transportation, the new order would make it possible for all members of society to use the railroads as they now use the public streets. The same would be true of all rail and water routes of whatever description. All that would be necessary when starting on a long journey (after satisfying the proper authorities of the legitimacy of your mission) would be to file an intention of the trip contemplated with the railroad or steamship passenger agent appointed for that purpose. This would insure ample accommodation and avoid misunderstanding or confusion.

Travel. Arrangement could be made whereby every person who had rendered his proportionate share of service to the common weal should have certain variable rest periods in which to travel and enjoy the scenic beauties of at least his native land. One year in seven could be spared from the labor of each individual in order that such a one might devote himself to legitimate travel and self-improvement. Does not some such an arrangement appeal to the common sense of you who read these pages? Men were not made for labor alone. A beautiful world calls them to enjoy its myriad splendors.

Individuals possessing more than one automobile might wisely be compelled to give up all but one of their machines, and permit the general committee of the whole to redistribute the surplus automobiles to those who did not possess any. Such a temporary arrangement would go far towards solving the problem of locomotion. Following this, the rapid production of motor cars would soon insure to every family or individual a high-grade car of approved construction. The same arrangement of giving up one's unoccupied houses — in the case of the very well-to-do — would insure homes to millions now poorly or improperly sheltered.

ABILITY

Under our existing form of enterprise the person who possesses the ability to make money is rewarded above the possessor of every other form of ability. This is a grave injustice. Just because my God-given ability runs to musical, oratorical, artistic, dramatic or mechanical ability is no reason why I should be penalized all of my life.

Because a person's ability is not commercially valuable is no sign that such ability might not be tremendously worth while in a sane, well-ordered, humane scheme of things. Any social system that purports to reward merit ought to provide a place and a reward for other kinds of merit than the common ability to make and hoard money. "There are diversities of gifts but the same spirit." By rewarding all according to their needs, regardless of their money-making ability, the new order would encourage the development of a many-sided and highly cultured state of society not possible under a profit-making and commercialized social order.

Irrational Rewards. There is no more reason

why the ability to make money should be rewarded above any other form of ability than that one color in the rainbow should be more necessary to a complete rainbow than another. "All are needed by each one; nothing is fair or good alone." Millions of people possess talents for which there is little or no market under the existing order of things, and are, therefore, unable to secure either recognition or reward. Not possessing the requisite commercial instinct to popularize their contribution to the world, they live and die, "unwept, unhonored and unsung," for lack of a press agent and business manager. The present system is neither fair nor free to millions of earth's people. The great number of human "misfits" is a living witness to this fact, and a scathing indictment of the entire system.

Greater Ability Possible. The coming order, by freeing mankind from the necessity of doing things for money, would liberate vast stores of ability along little dreamed of lines now crowded down and out by a ruthless commercialism. Ability is a thing which should not be bought and sold. It is degrading to men to be obliged to capitalize their talents. Nor should it be possible to capitalize one's natural good looks, pleasing manner or personal appearance. Inheritance and environment are so diverse, and the individual is, after all, so remotely responsible for his being what he is, that great injustice could be avoided by eliminating the temptation to capitalize traits of character, talents and aptitudes. There should be no price put upon genius of whatever kind.

Not the least of present-day evils lies in the necessity of a boy or girl hiring themselves out to an individual, and being obliged to look to that particular individual or corporation for favor, opportunity and advancement. It is socially vicious for one's whole future to depend on a private employer.

Society the Loser Today. It is not rational or economical from a social standpoint to permit the rising generation to drift into the commercial maelstrom all unfitted and illadvised as so many are compelled to do today. Young people should not be compelled to subordinate their whole individuality to the whims and fancies of those who furnish them with employment.

Who will say that it is right and good to compel a boy or a girl to accept any old wage a private employer feels able to offer, without regard to the social worth of such a boy or girl? What a loss to the world it frequently is under the present state for many a talented youngster to, through sheer necessity, be obliged to forsake the occupation or profession nearest his heart's desire and, instead, follow a line of employment altogether unsuited to him simply because "there's money in it!" How many tragedies result from just this sort of compulsion which fails to take into account either the bent or the worth of the plastic youth or maiden starting out to "earn his living."

Vocational Guidance Necessary

No individual is wise enough to dictate the life work of another. Only a select body of experienced and sympathetic men and women should have the say in determining the niche in which a boy or girl should render their utmost contribution to society. Our present hit-or-miss system of vocational guidance is vitiated because of the necessity of modern business to show a profit.

It is little short of criminal to suffer our boys and girls to grow into manhood and womanhood circumscribed and conditioned by the false and artificial requirements of modern business. Life-long error and consequent bitterness are all too frequent because of the vicious system of today. The new order would provide for the highest social efficiency of everybody by a careful, prayerful and painstaking system of vocational guidance. Not until the money-making incentive is removed, can we begin to realize our desired social

efficiency and deserved happiness as "members
one of another."

No one would deny that money has served
a useful place in developing certain desirable
traits of character in many individuals. Neither
could it be successfully denied that money has
blasted and unmade fully as many characters
as it ever benefited. Since the benefits derived
from money have not averaged very commend-
ably, why not give place to an arrangement
whereby the average of human perfection would
tend to be raised?

Money's True Function. Originally money
had a proper and a useful function as a medium
of exchange. It made possible the wider division of labor whereby the world's work has
been done. To discount the part that money
has played in the evolution of human society
would be foolish indeed. The point is that
money, like most other creations of humanity,
has undergone an evolution in itself. It had
its birth in man's necessity. It was invented,
not ordained. And like every other human
invention, money tends to become obsolete.
No custom or institution of human creation
carries with it any guarantee of permanency.

To many people the walls of time and usage
have become seemingly permanent. Money, as
an institution, appears a fixed entity — something which "must be." Yet it may be that

money has served its purpose, like many a now atrophied organ in the human anatomy, and is about to pass into the discard.

MONEY THE USURPER

Time was when money was the servant of mankind. As a servant it was good and right. But today money has usurped its true function, and in place of remaining the servant of mankind has become humanity's lord and master. Because money has "had its day" and because "the old order changeth yielding place to new" already there appear to seeing eyes signs of its passing. The war is one of those signs. This book is another.

Whatever ceases to serve mankind in the long run is eliminated from the affairs of men. Because money has failed to measure up to the demands of a true civilization, money, like the Kaiser and his ilk, must go.

The Further Emancipation of Women. Another benefit of free access to the joint product of society would be the emancipation of women from domination by their husbands. What are known as "economic marriages" would disappear with the disappearance of money and bills of exchange. The much-lamented condition of "widows and orphans" would no longer serve to draw tears and donations from kindly and sympathetic souls.

Economic Marriages. Under the new order, a woman could have as many or as few children as she desired, and the State would be benefited accordingly. With the ever-present economic barriers to the bearing and rearing of children removed, a family life such as existed but rarely under the capitalistic régime would be the average condition of the race. With the reason for non-support cases removed, we should expect to see a surprising decrease in the number of deserted wives and mothers. With the great fear — the fear of poverty — obliterated, men would expand mentally and spiritually to an extent at present believed to be impossible.

A Cure for Celibacy. The truly pathetic spectacle of young men and women unable to marry or, if married, to have children, because of inability to support themselves in comfort and decency, is another of the iniquitous conditions which would disappear with the advent of a safe-and-sane Democracy in the economic life of a people. The inability of young people of marriageable age to mate is a terrible example of the failure of capitalism to meet the demands of a rational and natural community life. There are more than 17,000,000 young men and women of marriageable age in the United States who remain unmarried largely from economic causes. The future of a nation is not secure where such a condition is permitted to long exist.

CHAPTER IX

TENDENCIES

"Bigness" a Factor. The time has arrived when mere bigness is an important factor in economical production. Small, slow-going, private production is both wasteful and inefficient. Instead of making it possible for men in the future society to build up trivial units which bear the stamp of their own individuality — to the extinction of individuality in all of their employees — the new order will offer men a partnership in a world enterprise. What may be lost in egotism and pride will be more than offset by the glory of having a part in a world machine. Men's desires and ambitions — once freed from petty and selfish considerations — will expand and develop to include world service, with the attendant world-recognition which would follow the conferring of benefits upon the entire human race.

Signs of the Times. Already our best young people of both sexes are beginning to refuse to show enthusiasm over a mere matter of dealing in material goods. "Business" is not an attractive career for any young person with a serious purpose in life. For grown men to get excited over a mere matter of "making money" is a ludicrous and unworthy spectacle. The material basis of life ought to be run and to be taken as a matter of course — something which everybody admits the necessity of, but which nobody should allow to dictate his whole life's course. The main consideration in dealing with problems of food, clothing and shelter, should be to so provide for their steady and ample flow that society could relegate them to the realm of commonplace occurrence and not be compelled to think seriously of them thenceforward.

What is to be desired is a state of society in which the flow of economic wealth in response to human effort would occupy no more attention from society than the ordinary processes of digestion and nutrition do to the normal, healthy human being. Food, raiment and shelter of necessity occupy an important place in our human economy, but they should not be uppermost or supersede the more important requirement of mental expansion and soul growth.

Moral Tonic. For the general welfare of society every one should be glad to labor industriously for a few hours a day in return for all that he enjoys from the hand of his fellow men. Both from the standpoint of physical well-being and moral well-being every one of mature years ought to be glad to take a hand in the never-to-be-gotten-rid-of labor of living. The entire morale of society would be lifted and purified if all put their shoulders to the wheel for a short period each day until the mere matter of physical provision was guaranteed.

A new Ethic will come out of the war. It will be the ethic of service — of value received. Millions of irresponsible, non-productive people are finding through the war for the first time in their lives that it is fun to work! Millions more are being shamed out of their parasitism and smug complacency by the toil and sacrifice of others, and are discovering that they have been in society's debt too long without wanting to repay at least a portion of that debt.

WHAT THE WAR IS DOING

As a result, we find people who never had a serious thought in their lives steadied and sobered by the war. Many persons have a real, live interest in living for the first time in their lives. The thought that all that they have unthinkingly enjoyed is in danger of being wiped out as if it had never been, has served to arouse and stimulate many a butterfly into temporary usefulness. The reason why some people are so very "utterly utter" over the tragedy of the war can be traced again to the fact that this is the first really important crisis they have ever experienced. Hence their tremendous outpouring of nervous energy. Yes, the war is very much of an eye-opener all along the line. It has served to clear the way.

A still further justification for the change advocated (if any further justification were required) is the fact that a large percentage of the population is hopelessly in debt. Many never expect to get out of debt so long as the existing social order prevails. Owing to the war, nations, as well as individuals, have likewise become hopelessly obligated to their creditors. Many economists frankly see no hope of some of the belligerent nations ever paying their immense war debts. The nations which lose the war certainly will be in no condition to pay war debts for a generation to come.

Bankruptcy. Personal and national bankruptcy stares the world in the face from every quarter. What's to be the result? Instead of attempting to "square up" when the war is over, how much simpler it would be to cross off all the old scores and commence anew under the plan of unrestricted production and distribution here suggested. No conceivable benefit can accrue to the stricken and devastated nations to be compared with the uniform adoption of this sane and vigorous principle.

To attempt to return to the old competitive struggle after the war would be an admission of human folly and stupidity which would be sad to contemplate. The world must go on — not back — after the war. And no modern wizards of finance can do one-half as much for the rehabilitation of the oppressed and bleeding nations as they can do for themselves by discarding the outworn vehicle of capitalism along with the czars, emperors and kaisers of a bygone age. The one is just as obsolete as the others.

After the War. Those who predict industrial chaos and the proverbial "hard times" which have followed practically every other war during the capitalist régime, are likely to find themselves among the discredited when this war is ended.

Democracy, once it has been made safe by the combined effort of more than half of the great nations of the earth, will see to it that those who risked their all that the world might by made safe for Democracy, shall never again go naked, hungry and without proper shelter in a land of wealth and plenty. To dream otherwise would be to arraign Democracy as an offender against humanity in place of the emancipator and redeemer Democracy is proving itself to be.

A People's War. Because of the war and the demands of governments for loans from the peoples of the respective countries at war, a condition quite unprecedented has arisen. Because people have put their earnings at the disposal of their governments in the form of Liberty Loans, it follows that those same people have thereby become partners in their respective governments to an extent hitherto unrealized. This partnership on the part of governments and people has been extended more widely than ever before. The percentage of average citizens who now have a direct financial interest in government grows ever greater as the war goes on.

By the time Democracy is assured through the overthrow of Kaiserism in all of its aspects, the people of the world will, by the loaning of money, have their respective governments thoroughly in their debt.

With the arrival of a democratic peace, coupled with well-nigh universal exhaustion of monetary resources, no more favorable opportunity could be conceived under which to initiate the simple democratic programme which follows.

Instead of endeavoring to repay the colossal war loans — loans of such staggering proportions that the mind of man faints at their stupendous aggregate — common-sense demands that a general reorganization of society give place to a more democratic and permanent system of production and distribution.

A Question

Either some sweeping readjustment must take place or the generations to come must bear the age-long burden of a crushing and insufferable taxation. How else can the billions of national debts be repaid following the war?

After all, the old order was never very stable anyway. It never wholly met the demands of a rational and humane civilization. No one would contend that there existed the smallest semblance of Democracy under the capitalistic method of doing business. Is it not pretty clearly demonstrated that capitalist greed and love of profit was the direct and responsible cause of the present war? Any return to the status *quo ante bellum* is unthinkable. Democracy could not keep house with capitalism.

State Control. Because of capitalistic waste and inefficiency governments everywhere have been compelled to assume control of public utilities of every description as indispensable to the winning of the war. This government control, it is conceded by many authorities, will never be relinquished. Instead, the ownership of all forms of public necessities by the people will expand as time goes on.

By this process of government control, still another link is being forged in the chain of tendencies which point to the elimination of all artificial and undemocratic institutions — capitalism among them. Add the direct financial interest in government which has resulted from the widely distributed war loans, to the fact of extended government control of those resources deemed necessary to the winning of the war, and you have a combination which presages much for a Democracy such as was never before known.

A "Safe" Democracy

After the world has been made safe for Democracy, will come the still pressing problem of making Democracy so safe that there will never again be any likelihood of a recurrence of the present holocaust. Only by the elimination of profit with its train of viciousness will Democracy be made safe for all time. The greed which caused the present war must not be permitted to find justification for another. Not until " profit " is made impossible will Democracy become an abiding reality.

No attempt must be made to "buy out" capitalism. In the first place such a thing cannot be done, and, secondly, with the utter abolition of all monetary forms of exchange, capital would be left with nothing but "dust and ashes" when its money became useless and unacceptable.

CHAPTER X

THE ACTUAL PROGRAMME

Now as to the actual steps necessary to put this beneficent programme into effect. The chief criticism of most social panaceas for human ills has been that they lacked a programme. That criticism cannot be applied to the new social organization of society as here outlined.

All that would be required to initiate the new order would be for the existing government to set a date not too far distant when the plan advocated would supersede the existing form of capitalistic society.

Set a Time. The initial date having been agreed upon, a vast world-wide campaign of advertising could then be undertaken to acquaint the people of the earth with the merits and workings of the proposed system.

During the period of anticipation — so to speak — the government would be busy (under the present methods of doing business, of

course) in building factories and railroads calculated to meet the added demands of society
when the halter of capitalism was finally slipped.
The entire world could so prepare for the dawn
of the new era that in every country on the
face of the earth adequate machinery for both
production and distribution would be in readiness for operation on a given day. This is not
an ill-considered statement. Actual statistics
are available or could be easily obtained to
indicate in advance just how much and what
kind of machinery would be required for the
successful operation of such a plan.

Appoint Commissions. Boards appointed for
the purpose could take into account the number and kind of non-productive occupations
now existing, and, by a system of training and
education especially suited to increase the
usefulness of such at present unproductive
people, so distribute the available workers in
advance that each one would know what he
was going to do — the part he would play —
under the new system.

Consult Preferences. By consulting the wishes
and natural preferences of all those who would
be transferred from non-productive to productive occupations by the change, regulation
could be effected without causing serious discomfort or maladjustment. The same
thoughtful preparation of all the other de-

pendent and downtrodden classes could be attempted in advance if need be. Or such adjustments could be effected gradually after the day for the great change had actually arrived.

Confusion Avoided. The principal thing to be avoided would be confusion at the start. By beginning with the children in our public schools today — and the same suggestion applies in all countries simultaneously — we could so instill into their minds what was expected of them when the change took place that they would be ready to co-operate in the homes to make the plan an immediate success.

Adults, too, by the above-mentioned campaign of education, would know just what part each was to play, and could be safely trusted to follow directions if shown that enough and to spare for every one would be provided.

When the Day Arrives. Then, when the appointed time arrived, those who are now at work supplying the material needs of society, would keep right on with their employment just as if nothing had happened. So long as those now engaged in the task of supplying society with creature comforts continued to function as usual, nothing unusual need be anticipated. There would be no upheaval, no demonstration.

How it Would Work. All that would happen

would be that some millions of people — each one persuaded as to the bounteous adequacy of such a plan — would cease their futile and unprofitable forms of employment, which were only of benefit under a capitalist form of society, and gradually take up their selected positions of service in the new order. No friction, no outward or untoward signs of dissatisfaction would result. Every one would be so full of anticipation and expectancy that only good results could occur. Such would be the psychology of the situation by reason of a long period of painstaking preparation.

A WARNING

Every one would have to be warned not to consume more than he actually needed until the new order gained headway or momentum in its added task of production and distribution. But, so long as everybody except the people in for a change of employment worked along as in the old days, there would be no more dearth than at present — if as much. The stability of the new order would depend upon every one living as usual in both work and consumption for a brief interval while readjustment was in progress. This point cannot be insisted upon too strongly.

Stability Assured. All things being equal, the world would consume no more of anything the day following the introduction of the new order than on the day previous. Because society depends for its living upon about a third of the population who are actual first-hand producers, no one would suffer lack if the great volume of non-producers ceased work indefinitely, provided their consumption of commodities did not increase. This has only to be stated to be seen to be a fact.

Provide Employment. But the moment the new order went into effect the millions who would be liberated from non-productive occupations, or no occupation at all, would become potential producers. The simple problem then remaining would be to provide employment for all the labor which would thereupon become available,

Either by previous training and anticipation (as before indicated) or by gradual absorption and direction, these unproductive hordes would soon become factors in increased production. The time would speedily come when no one would be without some contributory form of productive occupation.

Increased Volume of Products. The volume of production would mount up by leaps and bounds from that time onward. Then, and not until then, would it be advisable to permit unrestricted consumption (within the bounds of reason, of course) and to commence to shorten the daily hours of labor in keeping with increased production and the gradual adjustment to normal of all forms of consumption.

A New Era. So, having done away with commercialism and all forms of money exchange forever, humanity would enter upon a new lease of "life, liberty and the pursuit of happiness" not heretofore possible in the history of private enterprise.

Questions. Questions of administration and government under the new order will be settled by the consent of the governed. The people can always be trusted to look out for their own interests when they clearly understand what those interests are. Under the present system of salaried officialdom, with its prestige, pomp and power, there is much pettifogging of issues and baffling confusion. Present political and governmental problems under capitalism are too big for solution. If settled at all, it is in favor of the rich and powerful. With all their windy striving our present-day lawyer-politicians have not arrived at any worth-while legislation. Such beneficent legislation is impossible in a money-ruled and money-mad civilization. So long as we have capitalism, no two persons' interests are identical. The worker and the employer never did have, and never could have, anything in common. Only the utter abolition of money and exchange in all its forms can prepare the way to real Democracy.

THE ELECTION OF OFFICIALS

When there are no fat salaries and padded payrolls for political office seekers, there will be no more acrimonious political campaigns. Then, and not until then, will the office seek the man. Under the new order the man or woman who sits in the president's chair will be no better off economically than the grimiest laborer in the ditch. Governors and heads of departments, commissions and directors of industry, will all be honored by their elevation to such offices, and their chiefest qualification for positions of trust and leadership will be their desire and proven ability to serve. The man or woman who has demonstrated his ability to serve society to the utmost, the one with the greatest passion for human service, will be elevated above the rest. But the material rewards of all will be the same. Society will some day recognize the principle that, as Pippa is made to say in the closing lines of Browning's poem, "All service ranks the same with God; — with God whose puppets best and worst are we: — there are no 'last' or 'first.'"

In Conclusion

But the Fringe. I am aware that I have but touched the fringe of the new order as it will develop. Matters of real estate, inheritance, education, press, religion, medicine, art, music and the rest can be left to the discussion of wise men engaged in such pursuits. I would venture to give my frank opinion concerning them all, were I not afraid of trespassing too far on the good nature of my readers. If what has been presented is suggestive, I am content.

Education a Prerequisite. I cannot insist too strongly on what I believe to be the truth, namely, that in education, and in education alone, rests the attainment of the solution to society's economic problems here laid down. Once people become imbued with the desirability and workability of the underlying thesis of the new order, the accomplishment of the result follows naturally. Only, in a Democracy, a sufficient number of individuals must be convinced of the feasibility of the idea before it has a chance of universal acceptance. All this I realize.

No one supposes for an instant that such a scheme could have been applied to society at any previous stage of the world's development. Not until *now* has the time been ripe for this sweeping change. The programme set forth in this book is no Utopian or Chartist scheme

similar to the Communistic plans advanced by
social visionaries in the early part of the nine-
teenth century. This is not Owenism or
Fourierism, St. Simonianism or Proudhonism.
I believe a more hard-headed and common-
sense programme does not exist.

Not Visionary. Unless these contentions can
stand the most rigid tests of logic and scientific
criticism, there is nothing to commend them
to the attention of thoughtful people. I base
my faith in their workability solely on the fact
that their feasibility is already vindicated by
what the war has demonstrated, coupled with
the utter and complete inadequacy of the existing capitalistic order. There is not a single
sentimental consideration in my thought.
Every thesis herein expounded I believe to be
the most practical, direct and economical way
to secure to society the justly deserved benefits of society.

IT IS COMING

Objections without number will probably be
offered, and attempts will be made to discredit
the new order as visionary and impractical.
Regardless of such objections, I believe — that
is the important point — I *believe* the new
order is on the way. The war has unmasked
our respectability and greed. Henceforth nothing but the elimination of money from the

affairs of men will insure the world against future wars.

The ideas here advanced are for all time. I feel the hand of prophecy upon my shoulder as I write. I want no other assurance as to the validity of my arguments. They are the outcome of hours of mental agony and searching. In the final abolition of money from the affairs of men I feel that I have found the remedy for many of the fundamental evils of society. The elimination of money is only one step in the ladder of human progress. Problems of a far more important nature will rise for solution long after the ghost of capitalism is laid to rest.

Man's Deity. I believe in the intrinsic deity in man. Therefore I can trust mankind to eventually bring to pass what is for the final benefit of man. The same patience, commonsense and faith which has led the world until now will "lead it onward still, o'er moor and fen, o'er crag and torrent 'till the night is gone." In that faith I rest. Mankind can and will keep striving until the Kingdom of God finally becomes the everlasting reality of life. That the future of man on this planet will be better than man's past is writ on the very stars. The struggling ages give promise of mankind's ultimate perfection.

" New occasions teach new duties —
 Time makes ancient good uncouth;
They must upward still and onward
 Who would keep abreast of truth! "
                              — *Lowell.*

Ingram Content Group UK Ltd.
Milton Keynes UK
UKHW021816130323
418485UK00006B/519

9 781377 369310